To [redacted]

Thank you for important words!

From the D.

Peace,
Benjamin

Praise for *Diary of a Daughter in Diaspora*

"This poignant book of poetry spans an expansive array of topics: Islamophobia, microaggressions, racial identity, misogyny, the Trump administration, the occupation of Palestine, U.S.-led wars, European colonialism, and violence against African American communities. In the midst of living the challenges of diaspora, readers also experience the joy of falling in love and the pain of heartbreak. *Diary of a Daughter in Diaspora* courageously captures the local and global politics that structure our lives today."

— **Evelyn Alsultany, author of *Arabs and Muslims in the Media: Race and Representation after 9/11* and co-editor of *Arab and Arab American Feminisms: Gender, Violence, and Belonging***

"Founas's poems illustrate her honest recollection of the hard knocks faced while being a child in America with immigrant parents—a lifestyle troubled with Islamophobia and sexism. However, her buoyant voice still suggests a belief in change through social justice and educating the youth...Founas proves that she is a creative and courageous writer that this generation needs. This book is bold, beautiful, and a blessing to anyone who decides to read."

— **Kondwani Fidel, Civil Rights Literary Award-winning author of** *Hummingbirds in The Trenches* **and** *Raw Wounds*

"Bayan's voice is necessary and poignant during a time in this nation when healing is revolutionary, a call to action. This woman poet's work is not a small voice."

— **jessica Care moore, Poet, Publisher, Moore Black Press, Apollo Legend, author of** *The Words Don't Fit in My Mouth, The Alphabet Verses The Ghetto, God is Not an American,* **and** *Sunlight Through Bullet Holes*

Diary of a Daughter in Diaspora

Bayan Founas

ISBN: 9780692158401

Cover illustration by Marlo Broughton.

First printing edition 2018, CreateSpace.

Available from Amazon.com and other online stores.

www.bayanfounas.com

*To those in the diaspora crossroads.
And to my students in Detroit who
exemplify resilience daily.*

FOREWORD

The following poem is written by my student Bri Johnson. It is students like Bri who have inspired me to write my narrative through poetry. This body of work is MY story as a young Muslim American woman.

When I say resilience, that is Bri. When I say inspirational, that is Bri. It is youth like Bri in Detroit that embody incredible knowledge and craft that we must not turn our backs on. When Bri graces the stage, we are all on our toes knowing her eloquent words are about to hit us with a blow. And she does just that. Every. Single. Time. She captivates us with her astounding imagery and vocabulary. Every poem she shares takes us on an emotional journey with her. It is for her ability to captivate hearts and minds, that I share one of Bri's beautiful poems with you all. I hope she inspires you as much as she inspires the rest of us in Detroit.

"Sincerely A Black Female"

Black is beautiful,
You are beautiful,
I am beautiful,
We are beautiful,
No,
I am not a nigga,
No,
You are not a nigga,
No,
We are not niggas,
I will no longer be called out of my name,
I won't get down on the ground,
Chest to pavement,
Nervous, Shaking, and Panicking,
You'll just have to kill me,
Blow my brains out,
Chunks of my mind all over the ground now,
But I bet you wouldn't even think twice about
it,
Look at who you just killed,
This girl is innocent,
You fear me because of my intelligence,
You make me a target because you're afraid
of my vocabulary,
I will no longer allow you to underestimate
me,
I insult you with my appearance,
You hate me because of my skin,
Statistics says nine times out of ten I'm
probably going to kill you for no reason,
But in all reality you're going to kill me first
just for looking,
I walk past you and I reek of the knowledge
you didn't want me to have,

I stole it from your secret vault,
You know...
That book that you said you would hide all
the knowledge from a black man in,
Yeah I took it,
Now you're left wondering how do I know
how to spell my own name,
I will no longer walk the streets all afraid,
A white man cannot scare me,
I've been through much more worse than a
little beating,
What else is there to be afraid of,
Oh, you said you were going to kill me,
That ain't nothing new,
You kill my people because you're afraid of
us,
You're not afraid of us because we kill, lie,
cheat, and steal,
You're afraid of us because you know we're
starting to grow brains within us,
You're afraid that the black man will get too
smart and finally realize that they are better
than what you say they are,
All of the people that you have killed are
living within me,
So I promise you cannot defeat me cause
even though I'm black you are beneath me,
My melanin women are royal,
My melanin men are royal,
Even though I lack the melanin in my skin I
am black enough,
I don't hate my own race as I straddle the
fence but my own race still hates me because
mama created an Oreo cookie,
I will not be defeated,

You will not conquer the satisfaction of
taking the smile off of my face,
Right now I'm just trying to find a peace of
mind,
They look at me with modesty like I'm not
destined for greatness,
So I recriminize to them that mama ain't
raise no fool,
I ain't looking for no handouts or nobody's
acclamations,
I'm indifferent when it comes to success in
life,
I have dreams and goals,
I don't know about y'all but I'm gone be
somebody's wife,
But I be damned if I let a white man come
and take my husbands life.

-Sincerely A Black Female

Bri Johnson

8

●

Nocturnal zombie,
You have me
tip-toeing sleep.
This is me,
deadly.

●

I peer outside my window.

Their branches and leaves
sway in the wind.

A dance of the trees,
like no other.

No rhyme,
A free verse.

A free state that one
dreams to achieve.

A natural state of existence.

A free dance.
Being one with the wind.

A natural existence
humans can never attain.

A few weeks ago,
my mother had my
childhood tree
cut down.

I climbed it.
I found refuge in it.
My second home almost.
A place to disappear.
No judgments. No worries.
Nature's way of comforting my child-self.

Nurture from nature.

An old Palestinian farmer once said,
Trees are like people.
They have souls.
They have feelings.
They need to be talked to.
Need tender, loving care.

We are all a part of nature.
We are all God's creations.

●

He asks questions.
Always.

I am a book.
He can't stop turning the pages.

The climax,
his favorite.

The conclusion,
my least.

●

Microaggressions

boiling

inside

5

4

3

2

coming soon

to an

~~theater~~ asylum

near

you.

BOOM.

•

They treat me like
I'm invisible.
Walk by me like
I'm non-existent.

Islamophobia is
higher now
than the week
after 9/11.

At street corners
I peer over my shoulder
uncertain of what's lurking.

Xenophobia at my window.
I've drawn the curtains.
This home is dark now.

●

For my brethren in the diaspora:

Come sit on the front porch with me.
Let's leave this country momentarily
and escape our harsh realities.

On front porches you can hear
my mama's loud Arabic tongue
down the street
calling her family overseas.
Neighbor conversing with neighbor
two porches down in thick Iraqi.
Old stereo bumpin' Marvin Gaye,
jammin' that old Motown in the D.
Aunties gossipin' smackin' gum so loud
carefree.
Girlfriends with earrings
bigger than your hoop dreams
chattin' goals of Beyoncé and Jay Z.

On front porches you can see the homies
passin' a light over heated
debates of Pac versus Biggie.
Thick clouds amassed through the
greatest talks of the greatest revolutionaries.
Dreams birthed of King mixed with Freddie
and Huey.
Mama snippin' fresh mint leaves,
we sippin' deep red mint tea here
as rich as the Mediterranean Sea.

On front porches you can smell soul cooking
that gives your stomach buttered flies.

Abuelas stooped low flippin'
handmade tortillas.
Uncles laughin' with their necks back flippin'
seasoned patties.
Khaltos dippin'
their nieces'
hair in vibrant *henna*
that you can smell for weeks.

On front porches you can see
hijabs, doorags, bandanas, Afros and kufis.
Melanin poppin' in our brightly colored
dashikis,
kaftans, huipils and sarees.

Each hour plays a different scene.
At sunrise, grandma pinchin' grandson's
cheeks.
At noon, mama passin' recipes.
At sunset, uncles slappin' cards.
At dusk, brother greetin' homies.
And at night, sister callin' boyfriend.

On front porches,
we leave this country momentarily
and escape our harsh realities.

●

Spiraling

slow.

Falling

fast.

BOOM.

CRASH.

Silence.

Hello?

●

Spring is a coming.

Joy, are you near?

Sorrow, why are you
still here?

●

Little naïve Eve
teasing my spirit.

Tempted to pick the
forbidden fruit.

●

Body aching.
Eyes red.
Mind hazy.

Brain dead.
Body dead.

Please let me be.
Leave me on my own.

Empty.
Exhausted.

Brain dead.
Body dead.

Where is my savior?
God, are you still there?
I need you now, and forever.

-Teaching in the hood

●

The words that
flow out my mouth,
letter after letter
dripping like
honey off these lips.

As sweet as the
peak of bee-hiving season.

A symphony of buzzing.

Your ears ring from the
sweet vowels and consonants
blending together in
melodic harmonies.

Making every working bee
bow down to its Queen Bee.

Letters so
sweet and sticky
leaving you stuck
to every word that
escapes this Queen's
art of an intellect.

Making you come back
in swarms for more
of this sweet honey.

Like every working bee
who will never forget
who is their

Queen Bee.

-Poet

●

Tears by trauma.
Tears by laughter.

Every day is
a new day.
And I love it.

No one brings
me more
joy than my
beautiful brown babies.

Thank you for
accepting me
from day one.

Thank you for
teaching me strength
from day one.

-Educator

●

Jails create cells
to keep "criminals"
caged in.

Countries create borders
to stop "terrorists"
coming in.

Homes create fences
to keep "strangers"
fenced out.

How can our
gardens grow
in darkness?

●

Why do you keep hurting me when I stay,
but keep loving me when I leave?

•

I am the flower
that wilts in winter
and strides in summer.

I am the flower
that shrivels in shade
and springs in sunshine.

●

There are those who
enter my land,
bring me gifts of knowledge, wisdom, and joy.
These become villagers
who never leave,
never forgotten.

There are those who
visit my body.
These simply
enter and leave as they are –
tourists.

My homeland is telling me that
you are a villager.
Keep pouring your
beauty into me
and you have found yourself a
new motherland.

-Daughter of Africa / Your African Queen

●

When you're around me,
you just wanna straighten up.

You wanna do good.

I am your light.
I am your *noor*.

●

I shine brighter than your brightest days
on my dimmest days.
Spirit so holy you see
the light in me.

I drink that holy Zamzam water.
Spirit so holy you see
Lady Hajjar in me.

I lay me down to sleep and peep my future.
Spirit so holy you see
prophetic dreams in me.

I write with a thousand students on these
pages.
Spirit so holy you see
Virgin Mary in me.

I hold you tighter than fingers gripped
together
carrying drinking water.
Spirit so holy you see
the motherland in me.

I lift your spirit up when you're
too tired to carry yours.
Spirit so holy you see
God in me.

●

The Quran is divine
poetry passed
from
generation to generation.

The Bible its
mama.

The Torah its
grandmama.

-The Holy Scriptures

●

How do I tell a student
violence is not the answer
when he draws
stick figures with guns.
Girlfriend shouting,
Bae, nooo.
Corner of 7 mile,
a gas station.
This is what Detroit
means to him.

Why?
I ask.

This is what I see.

Guns.
Death.
Drugs.
Sex.

Distressful images
roll through
hour after hour.
Messages of hope
sprinkled in.

That day was
harrowing.
Their everyday.

How do I tell him
violence is not the answer,

when police stop n' frisk him for
being young and Black.

How do I tell him
violence is not the answer,
when his mama
beats him with the belt
because the world hates her.

How do I tell him
violence is not the answer,
when the symbol of non-violence,
the reverend and doctor,
was assassinated.

How do I tell him
violence is not the answer,
when he sees his face in
millions of men
behind bars.

How do I tell him
violence is not the answer,
when he sees his face on the
nightly news.

How do I tell him
violence is not the answer,
when he sees his flesh cut out
by slavemasters' whips.

How do I tell him
violence is not the answer,
when he sees himself hung like
strange fruit.

How *can* I tell him
violence is not the answer?

-Educator

●

Wanna know what I hate?
How much white people glorify Malala
but don't know shit about American
terrorism in Pakistan or Afghanistan.

Wanna know what America
doesn't want you to know?
Those terrorists they claim to be fighting
were birthed by the
masterminds of terrorism
that we call
"The American government."

Imagine stepping off your
front porch to the sight of
American tanks on your block.
Walking to school
passing a parade
of American soldiers
brandishing their egotistical barrels.
Sleeping to the sound of
American dollars dropping
craters the size of America's ego.

But you're too busy posting #yasMalala.
we've had enough of your white saving.
step back with your white feminism
before I clap BACK with
my black and third world feminism.

Innocent Malala blinded by
her own puppet strings
but behind those curtains are

the directors of true terrorism
brainwashing more of you
to steal more brown land.

●

I tell you I am African.
You wonder if I'm Black.
Don't you know
the white man created race
to separate me and you.

We are all children of Mama Africa.

●

The bubble tells me I'm white.
9/11 tells me I'm brown.
Africa tells me I'm black.
My Arabic tells me I'm arab.

-Daughter of the Diaspora

●

I tell you I am from Algeria.

Ask me one more time if I speak French.

Fuck no.

Excuse my French.

●

Dear God,

I will remain steadfast in
my fast to you.
These 30 days
unlike any testament
of the 365.

I lay here at
night and ponder.
Will I survive
another day?
Yet another test in
my faith to you,
Oh Lord.

It is you who nourishes me
in my weakest moments.
It is you who nourishes me
in my strongest moments.

-Ramadan

●

To my queens
who teach me and
inspire me everyday.

For
Angela, Assata,
Yuna, Maya,
Alicia, Beyoncé,
Abrar, Mama.

●

You claim the title feminist

yet degrade your fellow sisters

in hushed whispers

and cold stares.

●

Skin glowin' like the
Jackson 5 in '69.
Natural face
hair braided
Alicia Keys fine.
Your daily dose
of sunshine.
I'm on that
summer time fine.
You like to
watch these hips
roll n' whine.
Got you prayin'
to this temple
all holy n' divine.
Got your spirit gassed up
on cloud nine.

Sit down with me.
Chat with me.
I promise you'll discover
that hunted goldmine.
Explore my mind.
Ideas shine.
Hit you so hard
make you blind.

When they ask for a name
I tell 'em get in line.
Have to politely decline.
Cuz I already got mine.
Say somethin'
and we go in on 'em

like Bonnie n' Clyde.

You know I'm the truth.
You can always meet me
at the battle line.
Angela.
Assata.
Not afraid to be
on the front line.
Mess with my bloodline.
Panther.
Canine.
Attack 'em with
my sharp mind.
RAH!!!!

●

Listen to my words.
Cuz I have a way with words.
Golden are my words.

●

SHATTERED.
Glass everywhere.

Drip
drop.

One
tear.
Two
tears.

I wipe my cheek.
Blood smears across my face.

You seized my glass heart
and ran away.

Boy,
don't trip.
Oh,
did I hear you fall?

There goes
my heart.

BOOM.
SPLAT.

And into a million pieces.
There goes my soul.
There goes my spirit.

DRIP

DROP.

I'm losing count.
I'm losing energy.
And now the queen
has lost her glory.

●

All you young women
traveling in flocks.
Stop wasting your time
chasing these jocks.

Take one wrong step,
find yourself in front of a glock.
Take one wrong choice,
find yourself knocked.

Look in the mirror
my dear.
You are
too resilient,
too intelligent,
too worthy
to get your
life locked.

Stop wasting your time
being a mock.

Just plug in those tunes
when you're feeling down
and listen to Pac.

You can do anything.
You are as strong
as a rock.

Don't waste another second
and let that clock
tick tock.

So wake up tomorrow,
slip on those socks,
and tell yourself
you are
royalty's rock.

●

Fuck Trump.

-Human

●

PROLOGUE:

My heart flutters
at the first glance at you.

When we lock eyes
my lips feel numb after
1 second.

I seem to forget the alphabet
1 second later.

Give it another second
and all it takes is
3 seconds
to fall back
in love with you.

Make me your Queen
and I shall
let you share
this throne.

With each other's
love and intellect,
we shall
rule this world.
On some
Cleo and Caesar shit.

Smothering
the world with our
enchanted dominance.

Grace
me with words
dipped in
gold.

Baby I'm a worm,
so let me wiggle
my way
into your beautiful mind
and read
page after page.

Page-turner.
Cliff-hanger.
A brown-and-black epic.

Read
as Queen Sheba
and King Solomon
seize back
the motherland
and her riches.

Gloriously,
we shall prevail.

Now are we writing
fantasy or reality?

Don't leave
any word behind.
Raw.
No filter.

It's a confessional baby,

so confess your sins
of longing and astonishment.

Written in stone.

I will forever cherish
this prologue.

TO BE CONTINUED...

●

Watch my sweet words pour out my lips.

Like honey dripping down its comb.

Sticky to the touch.

These words stuck to your mind.

I am permanently imprinted on your heart.

●

Will this be how
I suffer
the next four years?

Or is this
just the beginning?

-New ~~President~~ Satan

●

Letter To My Visionaries:

Blue is the color of my soul.

I say this with a
heavy heart.

Carrying the pain of dozens.
Your sorrow is my sorrow.

When you hurt,
I hurt.

I say this with a
heavy heart.

Steps slower.
Heavier.

Morbidly obese
in grief.

Trauma.
Anger.

Each story another
life line
attached to this
heavy heart
that keeps beating
to the rhythm of
sorrow n' blues.

Every story
another pound
weighing me down
to the ground.

A mocking jay
trapped in its cage.

Don't blame me
if you haven't seen a smile in
a day,
a week,
a month.

But this heart
won't stop beating.
And these feet
won't stop marching.
This spirit is in
constant motion.
In a state of
motherly love
that never dissipates.

Don't fear
my dear,
for Mama Nas
is always here.

-Educator

●

Lost I am with you.
Miraculously enchanted
like Snow White's cottage.

One look at you has me
cradling 7 inches,
like the princess
cradling her 7 dwarves.

But the way you starin'
at my curves has me feelin'
like a savage.
Baby let's roam
through this forest.

Get lost like wild beasts.
Don't tame that inner beast.
Unleash that inner savage on me.

Like the witch's red apple,
one lick
will have you salivating.

Make me disappear
into your enchanted forest.

So good
got me hearing animals talk.
So good
got me sleeping under your cast.

Waiting for my prince
to give me that magical kiss.

Wake me up so
we can do it all over again.

●

Eyes rollin' back.
Enter into a universe.

Fuck the space jet.
You are my air.

Let's connect dots.
Constellations.

Take my hand now.
Let's take this walk.

Conversations.
Moonlit paths.

●

Hoppin n' scotchin.

That chalk-walk talk.

●

Take me.
Consume me.

Have a sip
of this fine spirit and
replenish your soul.

Nourish your body
with high spirits.

Spirits of joy.
Spirits of affection.

Let yourself fall into this
glass of uncertainty.

One sip too many
and you shall be drunk
off this Queen's glory.

Tipsy.
Stumbling.
Fumbling.

Lose control of your words.

Let your soul free fall
into this deep abyss
we call love.

Like butterflies
we shall roam
freely,

beautifully.

A caterpillar
no more.
Darkness
no more.

Don't be afraid
to let go and fly.

My throne
shall catch you.
My crown
shall save you.

Taste my royalty.
Feel high and mighty
off my energy.

I shall raise your
spirits to the heavens.

Keep sipping baby.
Don't be afraid.

You now have
wings of glory.

-Your African Queen

●

I love you still
lingers on my lips
when I am with
you.

Just yesterday it
left my lips
between each breath.

Excuse me if they
slip out words that
are taboo now.

I find my fingers
crawling towards
your warm hands,
catching them before
it's too late.

My body is still adjusting
to this muffled love.

●

These Sunday stars
seem to startle my stream
of consciousness.

I turn to your
warm brown eyes.
Brush my fingers across your
golden brown face.

Baby I'm scared,
I tell you.

How much longer
can this grin continue
before it fades along
with the bittersweet memories?

You ask me if I'm happy
and I keep saying,
yes baby.
Pretending like
everything's gonna be alright.

Hot summer sand
that burns to the touch.
Will this lead me to
blue bereavements or
wet wonderlands?

A saturated solution
of ambiguous ambition.
A white moth
dancing with the butterfly.

Unforeseen juxtapositions.
Yet beautifully dangerous.
Like Malcolm and Frieda.

A hero for his people,
the kids tell him,
keep doing you big bro.
Not afraid to
stand up and rise
by any means necessary.

She,
a gardener.
Growing an army of
melanated Kings and Queens
destined for greatness.
Feeding them the
fruit of consciousness
in a country that's waiting to
encage them
by generations.
But their royalty
cannot be seized
when it survives
through their DNA.

I bring my hand
up to your lips.
You kiss the back of it softly.

All of our complexities
are as intricate as the
webbing of our fingers.

On your back porch
you hold me like

the rubbing of
mama's hands on my belly
when I had a stomachache.

Your touch
fills me with warmth
like the lighting of fireflies
filling this dark night.

You tell me
you love to
see me smile like a
sweet summer day
in Belle Isle.

I take your head
and hold it
on my chest.
Bringing you back
to your grandmama's sweet loving.

My fingers gently
brush back and
forth from your
eyebrows to your hairline.
Brushing away the pain of
abuse and incarceration.

I nourish that
spirit with soul food
that your mama
didn't have time
to feed you.

thump thump
thump thump

Your ears
to my heart.
Your head
turns up to me.

Baby,
you say,
everything's gonna be alright.

●

بِالرُّوح بِالدَّم نَفْدِيكِي يَا فِلِسْطِين

With our souls and with our blood,

we will free you Palestine.

●

She inhales.
She exhales.

Stories of struggle, sexism, and survival.
In sync they breathe.
Across 7 seas.
Now let me narrate
the lives of these ladies.

Little Noor learns
to throw stones at tanks
before she learns
to count to ten.

By 5,
her father warns her
not to flinch at the sight of IDF soldiers.

By 10,
she learns the definition of
apartheid
by stopping at checkpoints everyday
where she has witnessed birth given
by new mothers
and dead mothers.

By 15,
her cousin teaches her
to stare soldiers in the face at protests
and that milk is the remedy of pepper spray.
She learns how
to run
when soldiers start chasing her

for fear of being indefinitely detained
or worse
shot by rubber bullets
that are not always rubber.

By 20,
she realizes
that Israel has convinced the world
that she is indeed the terrorist.
For being Arab?
Or for resisting an apartheid state?
You tell me.

Now why they callin'
a colonial occupation a conflict?
Like the streets of Detroit in 1967.
Whey they callin'
a rebellion
a race riot?

From the Gaza Strip to Detroit.
More brown and black hands behind bars.
Capitalism's black plague
shadows the north star.

She inhales.
She exhales.

Stories of struggle, sexism, and survival.
In sync they breathe.
Across 7 seas.
Now let me tell you
the story of Khadijah
from the D.

Little Khadijah learns

to duck inside her own home
before she learns
to spell gunshots.

By 5,
her father warns her
not to flinch at the sight of police.

By 10,
she learns the definition of
racism
when her teacher does not believe
she's read all seven Harry Potters.

By 15,
her cousin teaches her
that she is seen as a hoe
before she is seen as a woman.
She learns how
to 1, 2 punch
so the next time her
uncle puts his hands on her
she can be
the survivor
and not the victim.

By 20,
she realizes
that America feeds her left overs
if there's even anything left over.
For being Black?
For being a woman?
Or for wearing a hijab?
You tell me.

Stories of struggle, sexism, and survival.

In sync they breathe.
Across 7 seas.
Now recognize her resiliency.
And still she breathes.

She inhales.
She exhales.

-Warriors

●

grandmothers / جَدّة

grandfathers / جَدّ

aunties / خالة / عَمّة

uncles / عَمّ / خال

cousins / ابْن أو بِنْت العَمّ أو الخال

Tell me what those are like.

- First Generation

●

Dear Misogyny,

Are you really listening to me?

Or are you just staring at my lips
and blocking out
the beautiful words
that they have
to say?

Are you just staring
at the pinkness of my lips
and the whiteness of my teeth?

Continue to stare
as a black hole grows
deep within
an ever expanding
vortex of ignorance.

So now are you listening,
or are you still staring?

Take note in the way
my mouth mirrors
every emotion
in my eyes.
The way
they rhythmically
move and flow
with every letter that it
articulates.
Notice

its majestic shape
as it narrates
words of the spirit and intellect.

You see,
my lips have many
beautiful things to say
but you won't hear them
if you
simply
stare.

I promise
you will find more
geometric theorems
in the shapes of my words
than in the
curves of my body.

Open your ears
to my sweet domineering
symphonies of wisdom.
Making them ring
'till you crumble down
to your knees
in sweet agony.

I am not your
porcelain doll with
glass skin,
glass eyes, and
glass lips.

My skin radiates the spirit.
My eyes flutter the soul.
And my lips,

my lips move.
And they have beautiful things to say.

●

That ego can't fit us.
The creator of my stress.

So godly with those hands.
The healer of my stress.

●

You cast down storms of pleasure.
You cast down thunders of laughter.

You cast down storms of pain.
You cast down thunders of wails.

●

Gliding across the board
with a purpose.

They see my very aura
is royal.
Little Princess Aurora
has much to learn.

Cuz I got a plan that will keep
me movin' in my sleep.

That beauty
rest is for the weak.

Who needs sleep,
when my skin
is so gold got
your eyes blindin'.

I seized
those riches in your sleep.

You sleep
your life away waiting for prince.
A Queen never waits.

I am almighty.
I foresee visions.

Maleficent doesn't know what's comin'.
She thinks I'm out here sleepin'
like the rest of you folk.

Didn't anyone warn her?

The Queen is advancing
with a purpose.

Checkmate.

●

For Son of Africa / African King:

I breathe into you
like the Nile flowing through the motherland.
Blue creeks rushing aside golden brown sand
like your skin.
So radiant.

●

I'm hypnotized
by the white doves
circling above
our heads.

That's Allah right there
tellin' us
we are all God's children.
Tellin' us
we are fountains of peace.

A fountain bubbling over
with our tears.

Enough to keep us
hydrated for years.
Enough to keep us
drowning in our fears.

Allah, please
don't you see us down here
on our knees?

So numb in our feels.

●

نسا المقاومة
Women of the resistance.

Combatants and spies.
Nurses and cooks.

Djamila Bouhired.
Revolutionary.

Hijabs concealed weapons.
Carried concealed communications.

Right under French noses.
Covert operations.

نسا المقاومة
Women of the resistance.

Survive through my blood.

-Algerian Revolution / Daughter of the
Diaspora

●

What are you?

Are you asking to accept me?
Or to reject me?
Or to hate me
before even getting to know me?

Footsteps uneasy.
You eye my hijab so apprehensively.
Fear in your eyes.
I can smell your weakness.

My African roots make you uneasy.
Arabic tongue got you running.
Just like it should.

نسا المقاومة
Woman of the resistance.

You fear my existence.
Quite frankly,
your fear gives me fulfillment.
And your phobia is my nourishment

This hijab scares you.
Just like it should.

Your white textbooks like to misconstrue.
Got history all backward.
Please write one more word.
I'm that bomb you've been waiting for.

See me as the ticking time

bomb fresh out of a mine.
Yeah I'm the mothafuckin'
bomb so take a seat,
and let my words
blow your mind.
With these facts all aligned.
Got your
brains in my hand.
Now who's in command?

I've seized the power
in books you can't decipher.

Go n' tell Trump.
This hijab is carrying WMDs.
And I ain't keepin' it on the hush.
I've got Words of Mass Destruction
hidden in these headwraps.
My intellect so beautifully wrapped.
No wonder you can't help but desire.

I'm strapped with explosive beauty
that will blow your mind away.
I'm not talkin'
that superficial shit.
I'm talkin
that high key intellectual shit.
That
what the fuck she talkin' bout! shit.

I may be small.
But I got a voice
full of fire.
Cuz I'm a
legendary educator,
visionary writer,

suicide fighter,
exotic desire.
I live and breathe
everything that
makes you perspire.

I see now why you're shook.
This hijab scares you.
Just like it should.

•

In Algerian gatherings,
I am too American.

In American gatherings,
I am too Arab.

In Arab gatherings,
I am too African.

In Black gatherings,
I am too foreign.

Where do I belong?

-Daughter of the Diaspora

●

Mosques getting bombed post 9/11.
While 1 in 3 black men
will be incarcerated in their lifetime.

See me in a hijab.
See him in a hoodie.
See brown skin.
See black skin.
So they fill us in
cells and coffins.

War on drugs.
War on terror.
Same difference.
They just want us locked up
based on a racist system of error.
Replacing schools with prisons.
Books with chains.
From Guantanamo to Abu Ghraib.
More people under surveillance
than those enslaved.
The new Jim Crow.

2017,
Nabra Hassenen, 17 years old,
raped and beaten with a bat.
2012,
Trayvon Martin, 17 years old,
shot like a rabid dog.

See me in a hijab.
See him in a hoodie.
See brown skin.

See black skin.
So they fill us in
cells and coffins.

Dear god,
I thought hell
came after death.
So please tell
me why this life feels
like a living hell.

Call this headscarf
an invisibility cloak
because all they ever
seem to do
is look right through
me.

Towel head!
Foreigner!
Terrorist!

Stop me at airport security like,
Ma'am you need to step aside.
Suspecting me as the terrorist
when more white men
have terrorized this land
than history can count.

Columbus called his
ethnic cleansing campaign
"finding the new land."
Trump calls his
ethnic cleansing campaign

"making America great again."

Colonial dreams birth
deadly nightmares.
Husbands watch slave owners fulfill their
necrophilic fantasies.
Capitalist horrors seep our jail cells.
80 Iraqis just blasted.
Afghani school just exploded.

Kylie Jenner
hiding her stomach
gets all the press.
This social blindness
we call news
is leaving our education in a mess.

See me in a hijab.
See him in a hoodie.
See brown skin.
See black skin.
So they fill us in
cells and coffins.

To my sisters assaulted on the daily.
To my brothers under surveillance.

Let us hold onto our dreams.
The only way to survive and heal.

I had a dream.
We raised little Angela's and Huey's.
Raising the next generation of
revolutionaries.

I had a dream

that we overpowered.
Let our hands join together
like the fist of power.
We do this for our people
so don't you dare stop and cower.

I had a dream.
Visions of unprecedented unions that lead.
Arabs, Blacks, Latinos as one team.
Eradicating the system.
Oh, what a beautiful scheme.
The most colorful dream of dreams.

●

Miss, my daddy got shot and killed this weekend.

Miss, my brother died last week.

Miss, I lost my grandma yesterday.

Miss, my step-mom passed a few weeks ago.

Miss, I just lost my god-brother.

Miss, my daddy died this morning.

Miss, today is the anniversary of my mother's death.

Miss, my head hasn't been right since my brother died.

Miss

Miss

Miss

Why are you in school right now?
Child, it's okay to go home.

Miss, it's okay.

You are the definition of resilience.

●

I
am
building
an
army
of
soldiers
that
will
tear
this
system
down.

-Educator

●

Lil' mama melodramatic.
Lil' mama melodic.
Lil' mama a lyrical mean machine.
Her hymns hypnotic.
Eyes easy exotic.
Curves crazy chaotic.
Skin sultry psychotic.
Ego eccentric erotic.
Nails notorious narcotic.
Body bad bodacious.

●

Sorrow Sorrow.
You're so near.

Sorrow Sorrow.
Why are you here?

Sorrow Sorrow.
My sweet little dear.

●

Those other pussies are dull
compared to the diamonds
between my thighs.
I promise you will never find
another like mine.

That's Satan whispering in your ear.
Don't you see him laughing,
rippin' apart what we have here.
His evil branding
has left my heart
permanently seared.

I have found refuge in the
surrounding of
my own hands.
Replacing yours.

I can consume you in my
hurricane of tears.
Drowning you in my love.

Have no fear.
I have poured enough
to hydrate your
empty body
for years.

●

You robbed my
spirit.

I am an
empty body
walking on legs.

●

The village is in complete
darkness.
The sun has gone for
days.
Desolate.

Heavy shadows tip toe night and
day.
There is no warmth here.
No joy.
Eternal cold and
darkness.

I am the
village.

You are the
sun.

●

I wake up to you.
I go to sleep to you.

I consume you in my breaths.
You are the very air I breathe.

You cut the lifeline.
I can't b r e a t...

●

I am the dark storm
rumbling in the rainforest.

You are the sun
shining in the Sahara.

My cries
run down the Congo.

Your laughter
beats to the lions' lullabies.

●

You cradled my spirit.

You dropped my spirit.

SPLAT.

●

Writing these words
means this is real.
I can't wake up tomorrow
from this nightmare.
This darkness without you
is my everyday reality.

●

I remember the day
I fell in love with you.

It was a warm summer day.
The sun was pouring its rays
unto leaves and lovers.

Your skin was blinding gold.
Jhené Aiko was blaring
through the stereo.

Your eyes stared up
at its glorious queen.
I took one look at you and
I fell in your arms as
I fell in love with you.

●

I wrote you through
these words.
You survive through
these pages.

Each word
a memory.
Each page
your essence.

My nose meets the pages as
I inhale you.
My fingers graze the pages as
I caress you.

●

Wearing hijab in a white school and white
town is like an elephant in the room wearing
a pink tutu riding a unicycle.
It's obviously there.
You're curious.
You can't help but stare.
But you don't acknowledge its existence.
Ever.

●

Protecting daddy's stash.

He was told to aim at the feet.

If they break and enter.

That's self-defense.

-Teaching in the hood

●

Dear America,

You are robbing my Arabic tongue.

You've closeted by *djellabas* and *kaftans.*

I silently watch your crimes.

Sincerely,
Daughter in Diaspora

●

A post-obituary.
I don't come to the cemetery.

I leave flowers on your grave
in my mind everyday.

Not someone I talk about
but someone I talk to everyday.

Baba, you'd be proud of your legacy.
We are truly legendary.

●

You tell me,
I'll call you later.

Silence.

-Neglect

●

You ask me,
Why do you wait for me?

I tell you,
I have hope for us.

●

I close my eyes and
reminisce the
sweet days
by your side.

-Queen Sheba and King Solomon

●

You still smell my sweet scent on your skin.
Stop for a long second.
Sorrow meets you with silence.
Sending you subliminal signs.
Long sigh.
You miss my soft skin.
Regret settles in.
You sing songs of my sumptuous presence.
The splendor of my essence.

●

I close my eyes
and sniff these poems.

I can smell you.
You are still here.

●

The dimming star told her,
I must leave now.
It is my time to
enter a new galaxy.

The grieving moon
glowed gloriously in her
gravely clear sky
as she watched him
fade away.

●

I bottled my tears for you.
Holy water.

Here for you when you are thirsty.
Spiritual savior.

Quench your empty body with devotion.
Hydrating memories.

No longer dry and dehydrated.
Nourishing love.

●

I carry a
thousand stories on
these shoulders.
As heavy as
the bags underneath
these eyes.
Dark circles
shadowed by
their deep trauma.
Every bone given
to the cause.
Did I give any to me?
Sacrifice
for the youth.
The Last Supper
with our
melanated Queens and Kings.

-Teaching in the hood

•

Goodbye to makeup.
Goodbye to desperate selfies.

Hello to the stranger in the mirror.
I am beginning to like you.

●

A woman's wails.
The ultimate
sign of suffering.

•

Why would
we split when
we can heal together?

Let's be each
other's homes.

Let's build
a kingdom.

●

You were my home
I came to
every night.
I found refuge in
your laughter
when I escaped
the war of teaching
in the hood
every night.
I found safety in you
when there was
nowhere else to run to
every night.
Raising melanated
Queens and Kings
comes with
bullet holes
to the bones
every night.
You healed my wounds
when the sun came down
every night.
You were my
sun and savior
every night.

●

When I am still,
I think of you.

I move,
to not think of you.

•

At 17
she left her home
and crossed ocean
and land to plant her
new garden in
new soil and earth.

At 18
she rooted
her first seed.

At 28
she grew
her fifth flower.

At 33
her tree was snipped
when her husband
was taken by God.
The man she came here for.
The one she left her home and family for.
The only being she knew and trusted in this
strange land that has yet to welcome her.

At 33
she was left with
5 flowers to water with
broken English,
no degree,
no family.

She raised a
glorious garden.

Her secret is in
her fingertips.

Those hands
meet the floor
every night to
get gardening
tips from God.
Those hands
make home-cooked meals
every night to
nourish every flower's
hunger to bloom.

Her garden is a mystery.
She is a warrior.

And the other flowers tell me
I am my mama's daughter.

●

The sound of the
waves crashing
saved my soul
from crashing
into a million pieces.
White foam
washing over my feet
cleanses me
of your pain.
Where the ocean meets the sky is
where I want to be.
Its vast body reminds me
you are not the
only fish in the sea.
The cool breeze
washes my body
in wudu.

Thank you ocean
for rejuvenating me.
Thank you ocean
for saving me.

My body is starting to fill.
I can breathe
again...

●

Every night
I light a candle
to burn
the hurt
away.

I read stories
to get
lost in theirs.
I write
to get you
lost in mine.

Nights are
for healing.

Thank you moon
for always returning.

●

The stars asked her,
how do you
shine so bright
in this dark world
every night?

The moon replied,
I am glorious,
and so are you.

●

Their eyes stare
in bewilderment.

They wonder
how I make *hijab*
look this good.

Headwraps are
the crowns of Queens.

I thought I needed
your touch to heal me.
Your smile to warm me.
Until I looked in the mirror
and found the answer in her.

●

An RnB record on repeat.
At day,
I replay our memories of us
still together.
I have blurred the lines between
past and present.
An RnB record on repeat.
At night,
I have dreams of us
still together.
I have blurred the lines between
dreams and reality.
You have left me
but you are
still here.
An RnB record on repeat.

●

You visit me
in my dreams
every night.

I wake up to
the memory
of you leaving me
every morning.

●

Ode to Tupac / Ode to Immigrant Mothers:

Tears of an immigrant mother.
She fears her
native tongue will be forgotten.
She fears her
motherland will be a distant memory.
She fears her
sacred religion will be lost.
Sleep only visits to haunt her.
Tears of an immigrant mother.

-Daughter of the Diaspora

●

You left me
because you needed space.
You still contact me
with little space.

How can anyone
leave a Queen's space?

An enchanted space
embroidered in silk and
stitched in gold.

How can anyone
resist this magical space?

●

I HATE YOU. I HATE YOU.
I HATE YOU. I HATE YOU.
I HATE YOU. i love you.
I HATE YOU. I HATE YOU.
I HATE YOU. I HATE YOU.

●

I didn't know the wails
I was capable of making
until you left me.

●

I wasn't sad
at you leaving me.

I was sad
leaving
the kingdom
we began to build.

●

QUESTIONS ABOUT "IT:"

Do you ever take it off?
How long is your hair?
Do you shower with it on?
Do you know what your own hair looks like?
Don't you get hot with it on?
What happens if you take it off?
How do you not wear shorts?
Do you ever let your hair down?
How do you survive in the summer?
You play basketball???
Can I see your hair?
Did your parents make you start wearing it?
What does your hair look like?
Will you wear it your whole life?
You ran track???
Do you have to wear it?
What if it falls off?
Are you going to make your daughter wear
it?
Why do you wear it?
Do you like wearing it?
Why is your hair showing?
Does that color symbolize something
cultural?
When will you ever show us your hair?

●

Your smile
is the Somalian sunrays
that keep my
skin sun-kissed.

Your touch
is the Tanzanian trees
that keep my
toes tingling.

Your eyes
are the Moroccan moons
that keep my
muscles melting.

Your voice
is the Sudanese honey
that keeps my
soul sweet.

Your freckles
are the Ghanaian stars
that keep me
glowing gloriously.

●

My Pharaoh.
Fulfill your fantasies.
Your Nefertiti.
Meet me at the Nile.
Play hide-n-seek.
Find me at the Pyramids.
Fulfill my pleasures.
Find my treasures.

●

I lay at night
thinking about all
the things I've done
for you
and wonder
how you
could leave this golden gift.

●

I write
to heal.

I've lost count
how many pages
I've written
about you.

●

I miss you today,
so I am writing today.

I miss you today,
so my cheeks are wet today.

I miss you today,
so this memory reel
in my mind refuses
to hit pause today.

I miss you today,
so I have not been present today.

I miss you today,
so I'm dreaming about your smile today.

I miss you today,
so I'm tempted to call you today.

I miss you today.
Most days are like today.

•

Classroom Chaos:

CHITTER CHATTER
CAP CLICKS
PENCIL SHARPENS
PAPER SHUFFLES
PENCIL SNAPS
DOOR SLAMS
BOOK BANGS
BAG ZIPS
PAPER RIPS
GIRL GIGGLES
HELP ME
MISS PLEASE
HELP ME
GIRL GIGGLES
PAPER RIPS
BAG ZIPS
BOOK BANGS
DOOR SLAMS
PENCIL SNAPS
PAPER SHUFFLES
PENCIL SHARPENS
CAP CLICKS
CHITTER CHATTER

●

You are mama's daughter,
they say.

●

These hands love you.
They feed you to
heal you on hungry days.

These hands love you.
They console you to show you what
love is on your lowest days.

These hands love you.
They rub your
shoulders after rough days.

These hands love you.
They do your
work after long days.

These hands love you.
They shake business hands
when you have busy days.

These hands love you.
They rise excellently by yours
at meetings to show you
what our empire
will look like everyday.

These hands love you.
They write for you everyday.

●

In Algeria,
I am a foreigner.
In America,
I am a foreigner.

A stranger living
between two lands.
Slipping
between the crack.

An outsider
looking in.

The
diary of a
daughter in
diaspora.

Bayan Founas is an educator and youth mentor in Detroit. She graduated from the University of Michigan in 2014 with a Women's Studies degree. She is passionate about making educational reforms in predominately poor communities of color. Founas enjoys writing, reading, and performing spoken-word poetry.

Contact:
daughterindiaspora@gmail.com
@thatalgerian
www.bayanfounas.com

BAYAN FOUNAS

IG/Twitter
@thatalgerian

Facebook
@daughterindiaspora

Website
www.bayanfounas.com

Contact
daughterindiaspora@gmail.com
248.514.6037

Available on
Amazon & Kindle